LETTERS TO MY FATHER

NICHOLAS TRIESTE

Photograph by Hudson Picture Co.

https://www.hudsonpictureco.com/

Book cover design by Charlie Jurgens

Instagram.com/chuckjurgens

ISBN: 978-1-7367796-4-4

For my father.
I will speak my truth, even if it hurts.

And I heard the voice of the Lord saying, "Whom shall I send, and who will go for us?" Then I said, "Here am I. Send me!"

— ISAIAH 6:8

CONTENTS

FOREWORD

I was really unsure how to preface this one. So, maybe for the second time in my life, I've asked for help. I asked three friends to write the Foreword. These are their letters to my life before I can write the letters to my father.

By all means Nick should not be alive today, but for some force neither him or myself have any control over, he roams this hellscape until he accomplishes everything he needs to. I've received countless texts and phone calls these past few weeks as he worked on this book while going through a breakup. His words breaking through tears, silence, yelling, and jokes.

While I haven't known him all my life or even a large amount of it, he's made more of an impact than anyone I've met (outside of my fiancé).

I met Nick back at a retail job in March of 2015, at the time he was my higher up and was very quiet, I think I may have only worked with him 2 times for the first month I worked there. Over the course of the summer him and I got to know each other's interests and hobbies, bonded over our different art backgrounds and ripped into each other on a daily basis. As we started to enter our holiday period at work our manager walked out on us. This essentially forced us to form a blood pact with each other to keep the two of us stable during this period. The idea during this period was that Nick was acting manager and would hopefully be given the position if we performed well. Fast forward to January 24, 2017, I'm at home on my couch doing fuck all, and I get a call from Nick.

"Hey, what's up?"

"Hey, I think you're going to need to cover a few shifts for me"

"O-oh? Is everything alright?"

"My dad just died".

I've always been bad with processing the death of people close to those around me. But I knew that the only thing I could do here was be there for him. I remember when he came back after not speaking to any of us for 3 days, I bought him some food and a Dunkin' Donuts gift card. I didn't have much I could spend at the time, but he needed it—I wish I could have done more.

More time passed and he was told he wouldn't receive the position he was working towards—it didn't really matter how well we did. I felt terrible, like I failed him in a way. Maybe I should have been more real and confessed what he was already telling himself "they'll just transfer another person here and cover the position." But I know he already knew. 2 weeks later Nick quit and I was given his position. At this point I didn't talk to Nick for almost 2 months because of the anxiety I felt over being given his position 2 days after he left. Not too long after this we started talking more regularly again. Almost every morning I would open the store. He would be the first one in and we would bullshit about something going on in our lives, usually about a new part of his body that hurt.

Nick started dating someone that worked for us while he was still employed, and I thing this was the turning point for our friendship. I'm not always one to have opinions on a relationship if everything seems normal, both parties seemed happy. Sure, Nick can come off strong with his jokes from time to time, but that's something the other party should be aware of when signing up for it. And it wasn't until Nick started having more and more suspicions about things that he felt like there was a larger picture than what he had been looking at all this time. I received a call sometime around the Summer of 2017. He told me she had been cheating on him. He was crying. Frustrated. Despite everything I've watched him go through I think this was the first time I saw raw emotion come out of him. I won't double down on a story I know will be mentioned in this book, but I will say that in a 72 hour period of chaotic events and plot twists, Nick and I were consistently on the phone. He was updating me on the situation and asking for opinions and advice on what to do. This chapter in Nick's life soon came to a close, and while bruised he was certainly not beaten.

Soon after, I left my job where Nick and I met, and as I adjusted to a new work environment, our meet ups slowed down. We would go on walks down the local trail once a week and catch up with one another, talking out or frustrations, conspiracies and what not. He started visiting me at work at nights for what I imagine was to amuse himself by annoying me and spouting non PC opinions in a very PC town, which I always humored no matter how much it would make me wince.

In January 2020, he fell ill for a month or so, with maybe a new symptom every week. (Turns out he had Covid). He came in one day and said "Dylan I haven't shit in 4 days" followed by another visit where he said "Dylan, I shit too much. How do I stop?" He's someone that has detected my life in the strangest ways, and it wouldn't be the same without it. And I wouldn't have it any other way

He's strange, and deranged. But he's my best friend, my best man, and an inspiration to me.

-Dylan
2021

When Nick asked me if I would be interested in writing a forward for his memoir, I was excited but also nervous because unlike him, I'm a pretty shitty writer. Furthermore, he doesn't really need an introduction, considering the way we met wasn't much of one but I'm thankful for the opportunity.

It was Mr. VanDemark's tenth grade English class, one of the only classes and teachers that has greatly impacted my life to this day. I noticed Nick didn't talk much, if at all. I guess at the time I thought to myself to be mean to him, because that makes sense right? Even now, I still slightly hate myself for being that way because he really is sincere and we get along so well.

Whenever we had an assignment in class, Mr. VanDemark would walk around and check each students work, usually smiling and cracking jokes to hide the fact that our work was garbage and he was doing his best as a likely underpaid high school teacher. (I would say overworked as well, but he made sure to let his students know that he would go home and play Xbox with another English teacher and not give a shit about class until the next day). However, whenever he got to Nick, you could tell how much he looked forward to seeing what he wrote.

Some times, I would deliberately walk past

Nick's desk to see what he would write that made our teacher so intrigued, but I couldn't decipher much because of his handwriting which literally resembled chicken scratches. I thought to myself what the fuck is he writing that is that good? It's not like I would know then, and I wouldn't until I found myself reading a copy of "Bettafish and Backcountry" on a Southern California beach alone a decade later. I brought the copy weeks prior to my trip but I intentionally waited to read it then because I could tell it was going to be intense and I needed the perfect setting to really embrace the vulnerability and emotions that would flow me like the Pacific waves.

Upon reading the first page, I began crying because of the heaviness of the subject matter, but also because it was relatable. It was at that moment that I understood why Mr.VanDemark admired Nick as a writer in the early stages; I bet he could see how successful he'd be all those years ago. In the midst of all the emotions, the one that stood out the most was feeling gratitude for Nick to exist in my reality and for the courage it takes to express yourself on the most deepest moments of your life. Although he remains a quiet individual, his thoughts are loud, and his words are louder than the crashing waves that meet land.

-Carolina
  June 27, 2021

If you ever get the chance to meet Nick in person, one look into his eyes and you'll know he's seen some shit. Nick and I became friends when I was around 16 years old. His dark brown, almost black eyes already held memories most people could never even begin to imagine. We bonded over music and a tv show, Adventure Time. We talked about our troubles a bit, but I quickly realized how different it was for him when he called me one night and needed a place to stay. We were just kids and my parents were strict, but they let him crash at our house for the night.

Since then, which was almost 10 years ago now, Nick and I have floated in and out of each other's lives. But, just the same, we have still always been there. Not too far out of reach.

Nick holds a special place in my heart, for some reason (there's not a lot of people I consider so special in my life). Maybe it's because of how genuine and honest he is. Maybe it's his constant drive for growth that I admire. Maybe it's because he has always been there for me. From lacrosse games, to tattoo appointments, my college graduation, and every break up.

As I said our friendship drifted in and out as life just happens to do. And when Nick's dad died, I wasn't there. I don't know how I could have even helped in a time like that, or if he would have even wanted it. But Nick is someone that I will never let go of, and I will always find my way and be there for him the way he has always been there for me. I am so grateful that he is a part of my life.

Nick is one of the most resilient people I know. Life has relentlessly thrown more than curveballs at him, but he's learned how to play catch. He's grown so much since we first met. And he's not going to let anything stop him from achieving his goals. I'm just excited to see it all happen for him, and be one of his biggest cheerleaders along the way.

-Erica
   June 2021

Nick and Erica, Death Cab of Cutie concert

WHERE DO I BEGIN?

I WAS AND WILL ALWAYS BE A FUCKING COWARD. I HAVE no self-esteem. I've built up all of these accomplishments to be proud of, but I hate looking at myself in the mirror. It has taken a very long time for me to be able to say that openly, honestly, and come to terms with it. Now I truly know who I am and have a starting point to make changes in my life so I can be proud of the person who stands in front of the mirror and stares back.

I compare my life to climbing mountains, something literal and figurative. I've climbed peaks, pushed my body to the my limit, and committed to doing things that people who I considered friends made fun of me for. Who would self-publish their life and depression in poetry anyway? Me. I'm that guy. And I conquered that mountain, became #1, and some days I still struggle with finding joy in that accomplishment.

What's my next mountain?

Myself. To finally speak my truth, even if it pisses a lot of people off. I need to conquer the addict inside me, the fat kid, the depressed guy, the man who by all accounts, grew up with a father who was in an out of his life. The angry kid.

Sure, I had family. Dysfunctional. But I felt abandoned most of my life because of the painkillers and mood stabilizers my dad was on because of a back injury. I let that one event really drive a lot of my life, and dictate my actions. I ruined friendships, and relationships because of it. I became too dependent on other people. Whenever they left, and they did, I felt lost because I put too much on other people for my own happiness.

That realization hurts. All of those issues are entirely my fault. I was handed what I was handed, and I wasn't prepared to face it, so I ran. Whenever hard times came, I ran. Because I am a coward with no self-esteem, and I didn't want to face the hard conversations I've had to have with myself.

That's what I'm doing here, having all the hard conversations in front of you. I'm holding myself accountable and airing out all my dirty laundry—my terrible thoughts. I'm putting it on display so the world to see, because that's what it's going to take for me to make the changes I'm trying to put in place.

The next pages you read, they're not going to be happy. They're going to be fucking awful at times. I'm embarrassed to write them, because it's everything. All my failures, all the ways I wasn't a good person, the horrible way I talked to myself growing up, and ways I've fucked up in life. Though, I'm not apologizing for it, because this book is me, and it's what I need to share to be better and work towards the man I want to be in life.

I don't know who said it to me, but their words ring true.

"Why don't you love yourself the way you love other people?"

This is the love letter to my life.

Me, 5, at Christmas with my classic missing tooth, and one of the few photos that exists of me smiling

2

MOTELS AND SUICIDE NOTES

Mom and Dad

BY ALL ACCOUNTS, I STARTED A NORMAL LIFE. TWO parents. One a cop, the other a bartender who got pregnant in high school. We lived in a two-family home in Peekskill, NY. We had two dogs, a Pomeranian named Nelson who was an absolute terror, and a golden retriever named Charlie who was more red than gold. He was gaunt his entire life. His hair abnormally long. He outlived his entire litter despite being the runt.

We moved into my grandma's house for a better school district right around the time I turned 4. I was different. "Special, quick, intelligent." The words my teachers spoke to me and the ones my family engrained in me. My dad pushed it further. He always wanted me to be the best. Not to do my best. *Be* the best. At everything. Anything I did, I had to do at my best, always. I still do. Everyone was competition. Football, school, hockey. All of it.

I lived in a small room at my grandma's house. A white tube-TV, a wooden bed frame with a checkered flag blanket. Underneath the bed I stored all of my Legos.

One night, my mom woke me up from their bed. My dad had just been shot at. As I rubbed the sleep from my eyes, we drove to the grocery store parking lot while I wore a t-shirt and white underwear. My dad shook and cried as he held me. I remember him in his uniform, his cop car idling next to our white Ford Probe. The air was cold, but his tears were warm against my skin.

Not long after this, my parents got into a fight while driving home. I still don't know the details of it, but it was the start to my downward spiral.

My mother made my father walk home. I watched him pack all of his belongings in a black garbage bag. He hugged me, said he loved me, and that he didn't want to live without us. Going back, that last sentence sticks with me. It was the first time my dad admitted to me his suicidal tendencies. I had no clue. Why would I? I was young. I didn't understand what he was truly saying. But I would before I left Elementary School.

After he left, he broke his back on the job. He got dispatched to either a burglary or a domestic dispute (my family still doesn't recall the exact event). There was construction going on at the house. As he walked around on Garfield Street, he fell into a hole next to the sidewalk where the construction was. He hit his lower back on the way down and broke his spine. I was 7.

My mother and I visited him at a mental institution, or a hospital after his surgery. He was dressed in a gown which would become the staple of his life, and a consistent memory of how I still remember him.

We walked onto the front lawn which led up to a red brick building. My mom smuggled him two cartons of cigarettes. I watched the other men and women shuffle around in their gowns. This would be the first time I began disassociating with my life. I didn't truly understand what was happening. It would plant seeds that life wasn't what we all think it is growing up.

Around my eighth birthday I stopped laughing and drew inward. I'd visit him on Tuesdays and Thursdays, and we'd play Tekken or watch Jerry Springer while he chain-smoked Newports, popped painkillers, mood stabilizers, and mixed it all with cans of Bud. My parents were always fighting whenever they spoke, and visiting my dad felt like a chore. The comments they made behind each other's backs were always within my earshot.

I just wanted everything to be quiet, I wanted my dad's back to be healed. I wanted him off the painkillers. I wanted everything to stop. Just stop. Because there was no silence in my mind, and school provided no relief. In between the bullying, and inversion, I started to find my escape in video games and books.

Everything had started to take its toll on him, and me. It was the first steps in his downward spiral which would continue for twenty years.

Whenever I went over those two days a week, he only pushed that perfection in me. We'd practice math, and the correct way to speak. If I joked around, and said something funny as kid's do, I was immediately corrected to say things the correct way. I started to feel like I was never good enough, and I wasn't allowed to be a kid. I started lashing out at everyone when I spoke, and used games as an escape from my reality that I didn't have parents who would mutually speak to each other, and one was going down the road that would kill him. In short, my mind was fucked.

I fell into silence almost complete silence, at least until he started dating another woman. Her kids loved games too, and I felt like I had the first sense of normalcy in my life by the time I went into 5th grade.

One day, I went to his apartment behind the fire-house. My sister's car was already there. He had a seizure the night before, and I walked into blood and copper. There is no way to explain what it's like for a ten-year-old to walk into his father's bathroom while your sister stitches him up in the kitchen and see something out of a movie. Glass shattered, blood everywhere. There was a bloody handprint on the bathroom mirror. The blood was so thick that you could taste it in the air. The smell stings your nostrils. It tastes like licking pennies with every breath you take. I walked to the kitchen, and watched my sister stitch him up, only after I saw his elbow through his flesh. The gash from the glass so deep, the bone moved with every bend. His girlfriend showed up and took me away to bring me to her house to play games with her kids. But the thoughts had taken root. I wanted to hurt someone, or myself, because it was too much to see and try to understand. The OTC drugs mixed with painkillers had caused his seizure.

He called me that night, and we talked. I wouldn't see him for another week, but he promised that we'd go play with the kids.

Then they broke up.

He moved into a motel down in Croton, NY. I'd visit him there my two days a week. The walls were made of fake wood, and it smelled of old water and mothballs. He let coffee cups and cigarette ash build up on the night stand. There were holes in the mattress from the times he had nodded off and the cigarettes fell from his mouth or hands.

He called me one night from that musty motel. He wanted to say that he loved me, and that he didn't want to live anymore. The only thing I need to remember is if he didn't see tomorrow, that I was his son, I had so much potential, and that he loved me.

I never came back from that phone call, and carried it wherever I went. For years. I don't know if I ever talked to my family about it. But here it is, the dark secret that I never talked about until I started writing this.

I stopped seeing my friends, and I went completely into that world I had built for myself. Full of video games, and books. My anxiety was perpetually at 100, and being around people who were happy and laughing only made me feel worse. I was the quiet one now—the weird kid. I only focused on everything that a nerd could love. I knew too much about real life, and the only way to cope, was for me to run from it. Fill my brain with anything that I could. If I wasn't good enough of a son to make my dad want to stay alive, how good was I? That's the logic I had.

I would stay up for hours at night, believing that if I said fifty "Our Fathers," then miraculously, my dad would want to live, and his back would be healed.

When that stopped working, I got fat. Something I'd do multiple times in my life. Food and games became my escape. And by the time I started middle school, I remember my aunt who worked at the local deli say I needed to go on a diet. I took it personally, and whenever dinner came, I'd chew up my food, then spit it in my napkin so I could throw it out. I had no want to eat. I wasn't perfect. My dad was wrong. I had no potential. I was a failure. I ran, and became unhealthy. Now I was building bad habits that would also hurt me. All these things culminated, and eventually they'd blow up in my face.

To make matters worse, by chewing and spitting, I began losing weight. And I remember going into that deli she worked at. She told me how good I looked. I felt good. Weak, but my ego had been stroked. I stood there with an iced coffee in the 6th grade, and I'd continue half eating my food, half spitting it out, or not eating altogether. I'd continue that last part throughout most of my life whenever I became too stressed.

The rest of middle school was the same thing I think everyone goes through. The fights, the yelling, the rebellion. Except my life was all fights. Either internally, or with my father. My dad had gotten back together with his ex, and he lived with her again. He had ballooned in weight, carrying a stomach so large, getting out of bed for him was a chore. The pills went down like candy so frequently, that he would pour sweat in the coldest rooms. It was so bad, he always carried around a white towel to wipe his forehead with.

When my father moved back in with his girlfriend, I would pick fights with her children, cause that's what 13-year-olds do when you have issues. We took turns beating the shit out of each other when we weren't playing games together.

When my dad went out one day, me and her youngest started harassing her oldest, who was in high school. His girlfriend was over and we'd do anything to bother them. It was funny for us. A way to get a rise out of him, and we'd fight like usual. Except that day it wasn't funny.

He picked each of us up, and tossed us. Violence and blood had been spilled and we both knew it. We ran for the second floor, and climbed onto the roof hanging over the porch. It was the perfect hiding spot. Then it wasn't. He grabbed a metal pipe and I debated jumping, but my fear of heights wouldn't let me. He bashed my legs and when I turned over to shield myself, that pipe hit my rib cage repeatedly. Tears streamed down my face as flashes of pain overcame me with each *thud*.

He was kicked out that night by his mother. I don't know if my dad ever found out in his swirling world of painkillers. If he did, he hid his anger well. I never spoke of it to anyone. It was a secret kept forever. At the time, I thought I deserved it. My punishment for being annoying. It was a relief to feel pain all the same. A relief to my internal dialogue which was finally having its foundations laid.

My dad moved again, not to a motel room, but another house with his soon-to-be wife. I was hitting my mid-teens and our relationship was devolving. I was no longer allowed to visit because of her.

I called her a "stupid cunt" one day. It was a simple phone call of me trying to talk to my dad after school. She refused to put him on the phone. She was driving a wedge between us.

That was it. The nail in my anger. I wasn't allowed to visit my father anymore, and he continued to stay with her. I felt abandoned by the man I had seen go through so much, who couldn't emotionally be in my life because of his addiction and now physically because of his wife.

I am undeserving of joy and a father.

3
PILLOW TALK

WE CARRY THE SINS OF OUR FAMILY, AND WE INHERIT the worst parts of them.

Mental illness runs in my family. Whether it's unresolved trauma, or an imbalance, I see it on both sides. The depression, the anxiety, the want to run from your fears by turning to a bottle or drugs. It's all there.

There was something my dad was running from —his parents. I've met them a handful of times, and was always kept at arm's length growing up.

I never truly got to know my father before the injury, and neither one of my grandparents.

My dad, when we were on good terms, told me a story at his mother's funeral. The first, and probably only honest story he ever told me about his life. We sat in his green Monte Carlo after her burial. He let the car idle and turned down the 80s rock.

When my dad was young, he never had a pillow. Whether he slept on the floor, or in a bed, the only thing he wanted for Christmas from his mother and father was a pillow. That's what he asked for when they asked what he'd like from Santa.

He got that pillow for Christmas, and his father took it from him. No reasoning, just malice that my father took personally. I know he struggled a lot with both of his parents, but I know he never felt loved by his dad. That he was always inferior in that man's eyes.

He got that pillow back one day after a few family conversations, but I think that damage had been done.

Why would he tell me about it? Was it a way of him hoping I'd understand him? I don't know. But that's the story he told me.

I know he went through more than just not having a pillow, then having the one thing he wanted taken from him. I know there's something in there that he never shared.

My father never slept with less than one body pillow, and four more for comfort. His death bed proved that.

Like I said, we inherit things from our family.

I can't sleep right without being surrounded by pillows.

4

DRUG DEN

WHEN I GOT INTO HIGH SCHOOL, I STARTED HANGING out with the drug dealers. Maybe because I identified with broken people, or I wanted to rebel. I don't know which. Probably both. Definitely both.

Their house was loaded with bunk beds in the living room. I'd watch as all of their friends came over, bought heroin, and nodded off on one of them. It reminded me of my dad randomly falling asleep whenever I'd visit.

I remember the last time I went over, I went upstairs to use the only working toilet in the entire run-down house. (It's now condemned and boarded up).

It was disgusting. Covered in piss stains, reeking of shit, and there were rusted blades on the sink for cutting up all the drugs.

I stood over the toilet, balancing on two beams of wood as I relieved myself. The floor had rotted out, and I watched everyone sit in the living room bull-shit about their lives.

Is this what I want to be? Just hanging out in a rundown house watching people as I use the bathroom?

I wouldn't be surprised if most of them are dead now. I lost a lot of friends to heroin, but I am sure as hell glad that I chose to stop seeing them while I pissed in their toilet.

5

SURFING

My mom was engaged to an alcoholic. Someone I wanted to look up to as he took me out shooting, and watched the same shows with me on television.

It was my birthday 2011. I was out getting tattooed when I got the text from my mother.

Don't come home tonight.

It was the end of their relationship, and we were both officially homeless. I called Erica, knowing her parents were strict, but I needed a couch to sleep on if only for a night.

As I pulled into their driveway, I was talking to myself, bleeding through my bandages. They gave me a blanket and let me sleep in the basement. My company, a German shepherd, and a blind wire-haired terrier.

I slept fitfully, my self-talk turning to self-deprecation.

You don't deserve a home. You never feel right anywhere. This is the life you'll live.

My mother and I stayed with a few different people, and when I couldn't stand to be in anyone's company, I made a home in my car, or found another couch to sleep on.

One day, I called my dad and let him know what happened. He offered to let me sleep on his couch, but I didn't want that, I just wanted to have my father's voice comfort me. But, that never came. There was always that strong father/strong son dynamic he fed into, and I wanted sympathy, empathy, and honest conversation which never came.

I'd move into a bedroom in New Paltz, August 2012, but not until life kicked me while I was feeling down on myself.

6

COMATOSE

2012.

I got a call that my dad was in a coma. He had gotten into an accident with an 18-wheeler. I don't remember the diagnosis or what his injuries were as I left work and raced to Westchester Medical. I remember walking down that long white hallway carrying a fantasy novel I had been working on reading through.

The waiting room was filled with my family, all of whom came up, hugged me, and apologized. The chairs were made out of brown leather that you'd stick to once you sat down. I sat there, waiting for my turn to go see him.

I had so many reservations going in, that my dad was on his way out of this world. That this would be the last time I saw him, and I'd never got have a last conversation with him.

We hadn't spoken since I graduated high school in June of 2011. I didn't invite him to graduation because of the memories I still had from middle school. Him sweating profusely from the drugs and being entirely out of it as I walked across the gym floor. I was embarrassed to see him like that, especially in front of all of my friends. I knew the questions would come.

"Why is he sweating like that?"

"He looks really tired."

"What's wrong with your dad?"

I wouldn't answer any of them.

He took not being invited personally, as he had the right to. I knew it would hurt him to not be given a ticket, and I thought maybe it would be the kick he needed to get better. Now he was in a hospital bed barely clinging to life and I was stuck to a brown leather chair.

The doctor came in and gave the all clear to visit.

I stepped into his room and broke down immediately. The tubes came from his mouth and body. It was nothing like it is in the movies. There's a weight that hangs in the room as you watch your loved one's chest rise and fall with the beeping of machines that keeps the air in their lungs.

His blanket was moved, so I could see his insides.

The yellow layer of fat that hung on top of his muscles. There was metal wiring holding him together to keep his stomach from bursting at the seams.

I asked everyone to leave me alone with him in between tears and a heavy heart.

I walked up beside him on his left side, the clicking from the oxygen machine in my ears and the incessant beeping. His heart rate and blood pressure in front of me. Even in the hospital bed, he was still covered in a sweat that made his salt and pepper hair cling to his scalp, just as I clung to those brown chairs in the waiting room.

I leaned over him, and accepted the fact this might be the last time I got to see him given the circumstances. I couldn't say much out of the guilt of us not speaking. I took a breath and said the only thing I thought I could.

"I'm sorry, and if it's time to go, just know I'm truly sorry."

I'd visit him every day until he woke up. Between work and college, I'd stop down there any free moment I had, even if it meant going on two hours of sleep.

His dad never showed up while he was in that coma.

When he woke up, he told me he heard me in his coma dreams. He couldn't remember what I said, but he heard me talking to him. Though, I barely spoke when I'd visit. I just sat there, staring at my broken father with his guts ready to spill out of him.

We really did try after that. We tried to have a relationship for the first time in our lives. Between school, and work, I'd visit him once a week for lunch at Perkins. We'd talk, but it was always superficial. We weren't working on the issues we had together. I was too afraid to bring them up, and I'm sure he felt guilty about his circumstances and how they effected me. Then I fell in love, and everything went to the wayside as I focused on my relationship.

I know that hurt him, too. Because I was suddenly too busy. For the first time, I tasted that emotion that everyone longs for. He met my girl-friend a handful of times, but once our lunch dates stopped, our arguing started right back up like clockwork. Old issues die hard. And we fought back and forth being too headstrong for our own good.

7

CLOSE THE BARS

"I DON'T LOVE YOU ANYMORE."

That's the sentence that made me start running again. We had just re-signed our lease together, and now it was time for me to move out. But, only after I drank my pain away.

I took that breakup hard. I didn't see it coming, and for the first time in a long time, I felt like I loved someone.

You're no one. Who could possibly love you?

I was defeated, doing what I knew best, running from my problems and numbing the pain with cheap brown liquor. I was now a regular at all of the bars. I'd fly there after work, and stay until close. Even going so far to close the bars, find a party, and keeping my numb face going if I had a day off.

One night, I stumbled into the apartment I still

shared with my ex. I threw up on someone's front porch after a party, shuffled to the end of the walkway where I'd throw up again. I got halfway across the street, threw up. Made it to my mailbox and balanced myself. Threw up. Got to the door to my apartment building, and my projectile vomit hit the front door.

This is all you are. A coward hiding.

I should have been dead. My kidneys hurt, my body was running on pure caffeine to make it through the days, and if I wasn't drinking, I was sweating. I was self-destructive and should have died a thousand times over from the way I was living my life. My best friend, Dylan, he can attest to that.

I opened the door, covered in vomit. She sat on the couch, and her words rang in my ears.

"Do you need help?"

"Yes, but not from you."

I was resentful of our breakup and moving out the next week.

I went to the bathroom, and laid in the baby-blue tub. I continued to throw up on myself until I blacked out. Black out drunk was my ritual, my safe place where nothing could bother me.

My last thought:

Let me suffer. I deserve this.

Something clicked in that darkness.

I don't want to die, but I don't want to feel like this.

What's the point? I don't love myself, why would someone else love me? I'm not a good person.

In my mind, I was back in that drug house watching everyone talk about how shitty their lives were. I was exactly the same.

I started peeling sweat-soaked clothes off of me like a goddamn ritual. The withdrawals made January feel like a spot on the sun.

I'm sure my family knew something was up when I showed up to the annual Super Bowl party. I shivered and poured sweat, refusing to take my jacket off. My eyes were glazed and distant in the photo they took that year. And all I had to say was a blatant lie, that I had just gotten over the flu, and my cat allergies were flaring up. I felt like my father at my middle school graduation. Except this time, I was embarrassed I had gotten to that point.

Do we carry the sins of our parents? I absolutely believe we do. Otherwise, I wouldn't have gone down that road of partying, and drinking. I was repeating what I had seen all my years growing up.

There's something they don't tell you when you're scraping the bottom of the barrel. You're going to keep scraping it if you keep running. And I was in a full sprint as I tried to escape my past, and more importantly, myself. Boy, did life have something in store for me.

8

WRAPPED IN LIGHT

THE LAST TIME I SAW MY FATHER ALIVE, HE CAME TO visit me at work the summer of 2016. He was gaunt. A literal skeleton. He must have weighed a hundred and twenty pounds while standing at 5'7". His skin hung tight against his body, and the large shirts he wore only exacerbated what was no longer there. He wasn't the fat drug addict anymore. He was a broken and run-down man. He told me he was clean, and I never believed it. I heard the story before. I think he told me the truth that day he stood there as the sun coming through the window wrapped him in light.

It hurt seeing him for the first time in 6 months. We didn't hug. We didn't say we loved each other. All I did was talk about my job, and say goodbye. This was our relationship, and this is how it ended. As strangers. He struggled with things he couldn't fix in himself. From the abuse he faced as a kid, and the neglect he only spoke to me about once.

I understand him more now that he's gone. Because the things that happen to us as children really do get dragged into our adult lives even if we think we aren't those things.

Reflecting on this moment, him standing there as he came to see me, he was scared. I'm sure he knew he was dying, and this was his moment to try and make things right, though I'm not sure he had the right words to say what I would have liked to hear or what he was really thinking. After all, I couldn't give him the things that he needed to hear. We never had an openness between us.

I looked at his Facebook after he died, and he wrote a post that only reinforced my thought that he knew he was dying, or had planned to end it. I'll let you decide which, because I'm still unsure.

DECEMBER 5, 2016

I'VE HAD AS MUCH AS I'M GONNA TAKE. IF I CAN MAKE IT THROUGH THE HOLIDAYS, I HAVE 26 DAYS OF SLEEPING ALONE, 27 DAYS FOR ONE MORE SLEEP AND 28 DAYS BEFORE I AM AT HOME AGAIN. I AM SO LOOKING FORWARD TO THAT IN HOPES THAT IT'S A MUCH BETTER PLACE WHERE THE TORMENT STOPS AND IS REPLACED WITH SERENITY. GOD IS MY ONLY HOPE NOW, IF THERE IS HIS EXISTENCE.

He left this earth the same way our relationship

was. If I had gotten an "I love you" that day, or on my birthday, a hug, or the dad I wanted as a friend, would it have brought me closure? Or is it more true to our relationship that he went out on the worst terms we had ever been at? I know he still cared about me. But, maybe everything ending at our lowest point is more true than the things I wish life gave me. Why? Because it's true, it's raw, and it's not the fairy tale that we all want out of life.

I truly love you. I'm sorry that I'm quick to anger. I'm sorry that I don't know how to tell you that you talking about suicide only made me want to kill myself. I'm sorry I held you accountable for my own issues.

9

LAST CONVERSATION

OUR LAST CONVERSATION WAS DECEMBER 27, 2016. My birthday. 28 days before he died. He didn't call me, and when I confronted him via Facebook, it blew up—bad. I told him that I deserved a phone call, and he said I was ungrateful, and didn't make time for him on Christmas. He was right, I didn't. I didn't want to see him in his studio apartment. I just wanted to enjoy Christmas and not look my dad in the face, even though he swore he was clean now. I was being selfish.

Now, I believe he was clean, finally, but at the time, I didn't want to hear the same song and dance I'd heard over the years which hadn't been true. After our back and forth yelling via Messenger, he told me to block him because that's the only way we'd stop fighting. And I did. I blocked his number and him on Facebook.

I went upstairs in my childhood home with tears in my eyes.

"What's wrong?" My mom asked me.

"Dad's being an asshole," I said flatly.

She didn't reply. She knew better than to pry. It was a sore topic whenever it was brought up and to stop me from lashing out and yelling, it was just better to leave me alone.

I saved all those messages after he passed, a reminder that I fucking failed. I acted out of pure anger and hate, and what I got in return was loss. My last words were that I never wanted to speak to him again. And I never did get to speak again.

"I hope whenever you have a kid, you name him Karma, and you get what you deserve for the way you treat me."

That's my karma. My dad's last words to me.

That's a hard truth to handle, a hard truth to write, a hard truth to stare at on a computer screen while writing this, and a harder truth to share with the world.

This is my fuck up.

I kept those messages for years, only deleted them back at the beginning of the pandemic while I was stuck in my apartment. I couldn't bear looking at them any longer. It was and is my biggest regret in life.

I'm not a good person, and an even worse son.

After he died, I got all of his journals and calendars.

He wrote down that I blocked him in a cat calendar he kept. January 4, 2017. The day I think he realized I had cut all ties.

Nicholas Blocked me.

Clear as day in his own handwriting.

I still have that calendar, though I don't usually open it.

*"Nicholas blocked me" January 4, 2017 "Sick No
Progress Sleep Getting Worse" January 17, 2017*

10

"EVERYTHING FEELS WRONG"

I was home alone playing video games January 23, 2017. My girlfriend at the time was out cheating on me. I had a feeling she was, but wouldn't know until Summer arrived.

The world felt wrong. If you've ever been in touch with everything around you, and your gut gives up on you, then you know the feeling. That churning and gaping hole in your chest that knocks the wind out of you. I've always had it, but I chose to bury it all the times I knew I shouldn't have.

"Hey guys, I need to go," my voice cracked over their headsets.

"Why?" Ryan asked.

"I think my dad just died."

I drove around for hours. He hadn't picked up his

phone when I called, but it was late, so I left it alone and went to bed.

The next day, I went to work, and the world still felt insufferably heavy. Like a humid summer. My mind was someplace else as I wandered the floor.

I was taking a shit on company time when I got a text from my sister.

HEY.

THEY FOUND HIM THIS MORNING.

I was right. He passed. Gone. Forever. The words hung in my mind as I stared down at my phone unsure what to feel.

I was numb to the world, made too many phone calls I can't recall in the whirlwind that death brings. Nothing was real, and it wouldn't be until the 25th when we went to his apartment. That day has truly haunted my life.

My sister, aunt, and mother walked with me into his apartment building and waited to get into his room. Though none of us knew which one it was, I wandered the hall until I found it.

I sat down in front of room 3.

This is it. This is the one.

I sat there overcome with emotions I've never spoken about. The deepest sadness I have ever felt in my life weighed down my shoulders and crushed my chest until I felt like I'd stop breathing. Every angry moment and argument flashed inside my head. My dad died and the last thing we said was we didn't want to speak again. He told me to block him and his number, and I did. I acted out of anger, and now I was sitting in front of his apartment 29 days later from our last fight, waiting to see what lay beyond that door. It replayed on a loop for an hour while we waited.

The manager showed up, and when we greeted him, he took us to apartment 3.

My gut was right.

The sadness inside that room which was seeping out from the crack under the door came at me with a force that only a living hell can bring.

My dad's pink phone lay on the counter. His fridge held old spaghetti and meatballs he had gotten from the pizzeria nearby. The place reeked of Newports, and his dresser was covered in cigarette ash. A small Betta fish swam in its tank not knowing he'd never see his owner again. My dad's gray bedsheets were stained with blood and bile. His classic love for pillows covered those stained sheets. Next to his bed there was a bucket of blood from his bleeding ulcers which only helped end his life. He had thrown up blood until he finally closed his eyes for the last time.

I think of that moment more than I care to admit. In my waking life, and my dreaming world, I've seen his last moments replay in my mind over and over, and four years later, it hasn't gotten easier when that dream comes up. And it's not easy to write it down only to read it over and over.

He must have walked in, put his phone on the counter, and felt unwell. He would walk to his bathroom, or closet, and grab a bucket only for him to go and lay down in his death bed. He'd continue to throw up trying to catch his breath between retches. His stomach convulsing and squeezing to get everything out of it. The tears and snot running down his face. Only this time, everything that came up would be bright red, and the pain he felt wouldn't stop.

I try to think that in his final moment on this earth, he felt relief as his soul finally left his broken body. I like to think that all those good memories he had in his short 54 years on this planet flooded over him, and he felt love and believed he was loved. No more anger, no more depression, no more anxiety. No more suicidal thoughts running through his head. I like to think he died with a smile on his face, and whoever is on the other side greeted him with open arms.

I wanted anything to stop the pain. Alcohol, pills, women, anything. Just to make it stop and get my mind off of his dying breath. I was a year off alcohol, and I no longer wanted to be. Everything else, I did it in excess. And I fucking ran back to the alcohol like a demon escaping hell.

At his funeral, I wrote something from the bottom of my heart, and was the last one to read. I white-knuckled the podium as I stood in front of my family and his friends that I never got to know. I was crumbling. I hate being the center of attention, but I had words to speak, and I wasn't going to apologize for it.

Deep breath. In through the nose. Shoulders back. Chest out. Say it, or live with more regret.

"I'm jealous of every single one of you. I never got to know my dad the way you did. I only got to know the drugs, alcohol, depression, and anxiety. I have very few good memories with him, and what I do have, I keep to myself cause they're the only gifts I have from him.

We didn't get along often, and our last conversation, I have to live with that for the rest of my life. You all can pretend that he wasn't the way he was, but I knew a different man—because of those drugs and his pain.

I do love him. And if there's one thing to say here, he was all bark and no bite.

While we were cleaning up his apartment, we found two guns under his bed. And when the Sheriff came to take them away, he said they were only BB guns without any orange tips. We all laughed in that apartment amongst that death and sorrow. The last thing he gave us was laughter.

That's all I have for you. And I hope you know, that I'll always wish I got to know the real him that all of you have spoken about here."

I finished with Emily Dickinson's "Because I could not stop for Death."

I sat down and was hugged or shunned by everyone. The PBA came up to me and gave me a folded American flag for his service in the army and as a cop.

Just ashes and a folded flag. That's what you're left with.

After service, I stood alone surrounded by family that now hated me. I had set myself apart and probably hurt more people than I intended—only recently have I started speaking to some of them, and opening up about my life, and why I felt the way I did.

A small Spanish woman came up to me at the end of the service.

"You know, I knew Rich when he was a cop. He helped me through a lot of shit when I was a fucked-up twenty-year-old. You really are your father's son. He would have said the same thing. He wasn't afraid to speak his mind, even if it meant making enemies out of everyone he cared about. Keep doing you, always."

I don't remember her name, but I can see her face

and small frame dressed in a white-button down with black dress pants as clear as day.

My nephew Sean and Dad at his third birthday 2014

The rest of those days, weeks, and months became a blur. I was falling into old habits. I drank a bottle of whiskey a night, got up early for work, and sweat through my hangovers.

You don't deserve anything. You are a terrible person, and deserve nothing in this life.

I sat in my apartment and knew I needed help. I wasn't going to make it through this.

11

NIGHTMARES

I was alone with myself. My apartment was my cell, and I was drinking through the seconds of the day.

If my days were lonely, my nights were insufferable.

I've talked and written about my nightmares before, but I never truly went into depth on them.

My dad's apartment was static in my head, and the nights made it real. I'd be floating there, watching him pass countless times over. I knew I was dreaming. It's like watching the television but not being able to change the channel. I could never wake myself up as I watched the same scene play over multiple times every night.

He'd stumble into his bathroom, then back to his bed. He'd sit up, eject from his body, lie back down, sweating while staring at the ceiling, then repeat the process over and over while I watched from the dresser coated in cigarette ash.

It replayed on a loop every time his soul was greeted by Death and taken away. The bags under my eyes were a testament to my nights being my torture chamber.

I've always had bad nightmares growing up. Middle school was his bathroom coated in blood, and the night I couldn't wake him as he nodded off from the pills.

I must have been 9 years old. It was before he had the seizure. I woke up to use the bathroom. The bedroom was so dark I couldn't find the door or the lightswitch. I crawled back into bed with him and shook him. He never budged or woke up. The phone wasn't on the charger, and I went back to bed, hoping that he wouldn't die in his sleep.

On my really bad days, when the night terrors hit, I see him dying on loop in my own room. My brain still reeling from the nightmares creates his death scene for me. I've woken up in a sweat, unable to move, knowing I was in my apartment, but see him at the foot of my bed throwing up into a bucket —dying.

12

LITHIUM

I TRIED GETTING HELP THREE MONTHS AFTER MY DAD'S funeral, I was nothing. A shell of a person. I had quit my job because I didn't get the promotion I was promised.

Through my drunken nights, I pulled the store out of a deficit. It was one of the only two in the district to make profit for the year. Three days after my dad died, I got a call from my District Manager.

"I talked to the VP. He said you did good, but you aren't meeting the expectations of a Store Manager. You'll be going back to Assistant and we'll be bringing in someone else."

How the fuck can I meet expectations at a store when I need to bury my father?

I was furious. I gave my notice, then I started

working in a factory manufacturing pills for anxiety. I know, the fucking irony there.

I called my mom crying after a month there. I couldn't function, and working in a small white room around machines with no one to talk to all day had taken a toll I didn't want to address. I sat on my porch, and stared at my brown boots which had turned white from the chemical dust I dragged home every day and washed off my body.

I wasn't going to go back to work that day. I didn't know what I wanted or needed, but I couldn't keep a job. I never showed up that day, never called to give notice. I just simply stopped. My manager texted me the next week and asked if I was okay. The only response I gave was "yes."

I wasn't nearly okay. I was far from it. I wasn't eating, and I couldn't get through the day let alone an hour without having a breakdown.

I made a few phone calls, and I went to therapy.

It consisted of a social worker meeting me in a room twice a week to talk about my problems. Why I felt guilt, why I was depressed, and he always asked if I wanted to hurt myself. Every time the question came up, I responded with a firm "no" because I had heard all the stories about going away, and seen it with my dad being in and out of the mental hospitals. I was terrified that would be me. Just another statistic to a broken system that I actively hated.

You can't go away, you'll never be heard from again and that's worse than death.

Our last meeting, I told him I couldn't drive by my dad's apartment without breaking down in tears.

"You have some form of PTSD, and I don't think I can help you anymore. I'm going to recommend you see the Psychiatrist here."

I nodded in ascent. It was another defeat, but I held out hope that a real doctor would be able to help me come to terms with grief, and find what had been breaking me inside since childhood.

The next week, I went into the same office and was greeted by a woman. We sat there for fifteen minutes, and as we went through the questions of my lack of interest, depression, if I felt anxious, what brought me in, and me not being able to hold a steady job, she gave me a few words.

"I believe you have full-blown PTSD. I also think you have Major Depressive Disorder, and are Bipolar two."

"My dad was Bipolar. What's two?"

"So, with Bipolar two, your base level is Depressive, and then you move to mania which makes you spend money frivolously, chase drugs, alcohol, and sex. Then once you have satisfied that mania, you fall back to your baseline which for you is low. But with Bipolar Two you never reach a full peak for mania."

What does this mean for me? Am I just going to be like this forever?

The thoughts started swirling and my world was a consistent mess.

You're never going to be right. You're always going to be fucked up. You are *a fuck up. Just admit it. You're a fuck up.*

"I'm going to want to meet with you again, but I want to prescribe you Lithium if you still feel the same way."

I knew drugs from working in the factory, and from school. I knew what Lithium did to people. And it was not a way I wanted to live. I didn't care if I was broken. I knew I needed to write and create. A chemical lobotomy was out of the question for me.

Better to die who I am than a zombie.

"Okay," I said, downtrodden.

"Just go up to the front desk and set up your next appointment. I look forward to seeing you."

Fuck you, cunt. You're just going to write me a script and send me off. Just like the doctors did for my dad. Just like everyone else. Just written off. That's all I'll ever be.

I never walked up to book that appointment, and that was the last day I ever talked to a therapist or psychiatrist.

If I can't find peace in this world without drugs, then this world isn't for me.

It became my motto, and it set something in me,

a foundation for independence that I wouldn't chase for a year. This was the pivotal moment for me to travel, hike, camp, and survive in the wild. I had no clue, but that last meeting and the word "Lithium" changed my life because it terrified me. I would start searching for my happiness.

13

MENTAL WARD

6 MONTHS AFTER MY DAD'S PASSING, I FOUND OUT MY girlfriend was cheating on me. It was summer, and she had just come back to the area for school. We were having a rocky relationship, and I asked her to come over. When she told me no, that she was going to stay at her friend's house, I had had enough.

While she was at work, I drove to her friend's house and asked the guy what the deal was with her.

He said, "she's my girlfriend. Why?"

"I guess I'm her other boyfriend."

I showed him all of our texts.

I helped him pack up all of her belongings, and while going through everything that she kept there, I found collectibles I had lent her. She had given them to him as gifts, books and games worth thousands of dollars.

When she arrived and saw us both standing there, she called me a liar, and said I was ruining her relationship with him because I was the jealous guy she used to sleep with. Then she ran off into the woods. I went home after collecting everything that was rightfully mine, and did what I did best, got drunk.

She called me at 2am. A voicemail for a suicide note that said she was sorry, and that she was bleeding out. I had been the last person she called. I immediately called the police.

I said, "my ex and I got into a fight, and she called me to say she was killing herself."

They found her and saved that girl's life. But I got to spend the morning in the police station answering questions.

I was resentful again. While I sat there in the police station, all I could think was that no good deed went unpunished. I had been the only one to call the police, and after all was said and done, the same cops that talked to me in that police station said I was the only reason she was alive, because no one else had picked up her call or bothered to dial 911.

When she finally was transferred from the ER to the mental ward, I got a phone call from her asking to come visit her. Against everyone's advice, I went and did it. Told them that no one deserved to be alone at their worst moments, because I knew what it was like to not have anyone around.

I went every day for three weeks to visit her. And when she got out and we talked about what happened, it devolved into an argument, and she told me she wished her other boyfriend had made the phone call that saved her life.

We cut all ties.

Months later I'd get a text the day of her graduation that read:

THANK YOU FOR MAKING THAT CALL AND BEING THE ONLY ONE WHO CAME TO VISIT ME. MY FAMILY GOT TO WATCH ME GRADUATE TODAY, AND WITHOUT YOU, THAT WOULD HAVE NEVER HAPPENED.

We haven't spoken since.

I appreciated the sentiment, but still went inward. My trust had been violated and I didn't want to be around anyone. I was resentful for what happened and pitying myself. For months I never picked up my phone when someone called or texted me asking to hang out.

It was cowardice that drove me to isolate myself. A hatred for everyone around me. I wanted to live in that anger of betrayal, and sadness I was still feeling for the loss of my father. Even though I made the right call, literally and figuratively, I was hurt. I wouldn't date for years.

14

WASHINGTON

2018 HIT ME LIKE A BRICK. MY DAD WAS DEAD AND I was not getting better. After my trip to Alaska, I was losing it. My ex had cheated on me, and I felt alone at each and every turn in my life. My nights were the same as my days as sleep paralysis and night terrors gripped the only moment of respite in my life. I was reliving walking into his apartment every second of the day and night. Those stained bedsheets and the blood were the only things I could focus on.

I was lost in the seas of depression, and I was making plans to end my life. I just had one more wish, to see the coast of Washington, and hike up Mount Rainier. Because my fucked-up mindset said that if I couldn't find joy and clarity in the wilderness, then I never would.

I thought, *if I can't find happiness alone with myself*

*in the wild that I love. Then I never will. And my life will
be pointless.*

It was my last-ditch effort to find something
worth living for, because I was hating myself more
than anyone could.

I booked my trip to Washington.

I was hiking, and drinking alcohol like it was
water. From whiskey, bourbon, and beer, my
kidneys hurt and my stomach was a mess. I loved
traveling, and it was my only way to escape and feel
normal while I sat alone in the woods contemplating
my life and all the bad mistakes I had made. I was
reflecting on everything, and I wanted to be
forgotten by everyone, even God. I wanted to disap-
pear into the wilderness and never be found again.

I landed in Seattle, grabbed my rental, and
floored it to Mount Rainier, completely unprepared.
The redeye was uneventful and the need to go and
do something and see something grand was driving
me while those incessant thoughts still gnawed in
the back of my mind. I pulled into Sunrise, loaded
my backpack and ran up the steep elevation that
starts the trail out to the Burroughs Mountain Trails.

Living my life at sea level, the air was already
thin for me at 6000ft. I'd still have another 2500 to
go by the time I stopped and turned around.

I passed by everyone on the trail, and was one of
three to sit at the Burroughs and gaze up at the

majestic ice sculpture that eclipsed everything in my view. The weather was a nice 60 at the parking lot. And by the time I got to my final resting place, I was shivering from my sweat, and pulled my rain jacket tight against my body.

The start of altitude sickness for me began in my stomach. I knew the signs, but didn't think it would affect me. Why would it? 8000ft didn't seem too high. But I was wrong. My stomach started to churn after I took my videos for social media.

I barely got behind a tree and got my pants down before everything that was in me got emptied on that mountain. I knew the only way to get better was to get down as fast as I could, and hydrate myself.

I funneled what water I had left and made it back to my rental car, exhausted and beat down.

How could you be so stupid? You have no training. You're lost and alone on the other side of the country and you can't even take care of yourself.

I got off the mountain, and set my eyes for the Olympics. At least I'd be back at sea level, and could spend some time alone in the woods.

The drive was long, loaded with music to keep my mind on something other than itself. When I finally pulled over to sleep, I found myself at a bar attached to an RV park. I shuffled in to a sawdust floor and a chihuahua that would not stop barking at me.

"Will you shut the fuck up!" A woman's voice came from the kitchen to the left.

"Can I get a spot here?"

"You got an RV?"

"No, just a car and a tent."

"Sure, twenty bucks." She wiped down glasses with a rag while waiting for me to put the money up. Her dog still barking and running away whenever I moved.

"Thank you."

"Bathroom is on the side," she said as she walked away.

I parked and set up camp, too tired to do anything. I slept until just before dawn. I had to go to the bathroom. I walked over and let myself in. It hadn't been cleaned in God knows how long.

When I walked back to my campsite, there was a man standing there. My hand went to my knife. I was ready for a fight. My hair was standing up and my breaths were shallow.

"This your spot?"

"Yeah."

"Pack it up and get out of here."

"Why?" I was fiddling my knife.

"There's a mountain lion over there," he pointed to the woods just beyond my tent.

We stood there a moment. We listened for the crunching of sticks. There was a low growl.

"I'll wait here while you pack up," he said. Then I saw he had a pistol on his hip.

I packed up fast, thanked him, and continued on down the coast to Ruby and Rialto beach.

I made it to Rialto just after the sun came up. The waves crashed against the stone shore, and the massive rocks jutted from the ocean like fingers of old giants. As I walked, there laid a dead seal. Its carcass just starting to rot. I identified with that seal, just something on the coast—dying.

I walked further on, and sat on my backpack. I stared off into the sea. For the first time, my mind went quiet, and it was a true moment of respite. I tried to hold onto it as long as I could until a man with blonde locks walked up to me and said "hello."

He was dressed in a hemp hoodie that looked to be the scratchiest thing you could possibly wear. His feet bare, and his pants torn at the knees.

"You're not from here, are you?"

"That obvious?"

"Yeah, you look like you're looking for something out here."

He told me his name, but I can't for the life of me remember it.

"I guess you could say that. I'm Nick."

"Mind if I sit?"

"Go for it."

He plopped down on his backpack.

"It's really beautiful out here. Been on the road for ten years now."

"I just got here yesterday."

"First time?"

"Yeah."

"It really is beautiful."

"It is."

We sat there in silence and listen to those waves come and go against the pebbles.

"Well, I'm going to continue on down the beach. I know you're going through something and I don't want to interrupt that. If you want company, I'll have a campfire going down by that rock tonight," he pointed to one of those massive stones in the distance.

"Thank you. I'm heading to Ruby after this."

"Enjoy it. I hope you find whatever you're looking for out here."

I didn't say a word, just gave a half-hearted smile.

Ruby was littered with too many people for my liking. I stood there a few minutes, then got back in my rental and made my way further south. Dead Man's Cove. That was my final stop before I'd head back towards Seattle.

I slept in my rental on the side of the road, and the next morning, I made my way to the lookout just as the sun started to rise.

I was told it was called Dead Man's Cove,

because the way the tide runs, all the dead bodies from wrecked ships would wash up near a rock.

I walked down the embankment and sat under a makeshift shelter and stared into the sea.

The water crashed against the rock in the middle of the small beach. And, for the first time since he died, I thought I heard my dad say something to me.

"There's something inside you that you can't give up on."

Dead Man's Cove

15
LOOKING WEST

I AM NOT A GODLY MAN. BUT THE UNIVERSE GAVE ME something out in the wilderness. Unabashed acceptance, solitude, and silence while traveling, hiking, and camping became the only thing I looked forward to, so I was going to do it as often as I could. My sights were set on the deserts of Utah and Arizona, then the granite cliffs of Yosemite.

I booked a trip with my family for the desert. They'd stay a week, I'd do two. I got to spend a very long time with my grandfather as we drove through Arizona and Utah.

The Grand Canyon, Saguaro, and Zion.

As we walked through Zion, I knew this is where I was going to spend my week as I stared up at Angel's Landing.

You're going to hike that even if it breaks you.

When my family left, that was the first thing I did. I ran up those switchbacks. I wanted to get up and look over that valley as early as I could. What I got in return was crowds, and screaming kids on a field trip. It was the first time I had been to such a crowded park, I almost hated it.

While I was on the bus to the Angel's Landing trailhead, they mentioned that a California Condor had been spotted in the area. At one point, it was declared extinct with about twenty left in existence. After capture, and reintroduction to the wild, that number climbed to over 400.

As I sat at the top of Angel's Landing, listening to the screams and chatter I was running from. I found myself a quiet nook and watched everyone take video and photos. I was no different than them. I was doing the same, only I moved in silence as the ghost I wanted to become. A shadow swooped overhead.

I looked up, and there it was. One of the last of its kind. The pale head, the black wings, and the white underbelly. It drifted lazily in circles. I watched everyone as they chattered and took their photos. I don't think a single person there bothered to look up at the sky. We were all too busy with our heads craned down.

That's not supposed to be a lesson that we're attached to our phones, or to say there's something wrong with it. But, like I said, I'm not a godly man. Seeing one of the last things in existence in the wild is something completely different. There's a feeling I have not been able to describe well or find the right word for. I felt connected, like I was being given a gift for trying to find my way in this world. I'd get another at a resort on my dad's birthday. I had coincided this trip with it so if I had a mental breakdown, at least I'd be alone for it.

My dad and I used to watch comedies when I was growing up. The Ernest movies, but some of our favorites were *Friday*, *Next Friday*, and *Friday After Next*. They're amazing, and one of those good memories I've kept to myself.

I checked into my suite on his birthday. I wanted to treat myself, see how the other half lived when money didn't matter. I spent $700 for one night before I flew back to New York and went about my life.

As I walked inside to check in, I was greeted and immediately had my bags taken and loaded onto a golf cart while I talked to the man at reception.

"You'll be at the other end of the resort with a great view of the mountain."

"Okay, thank you," I said as I took my keys and went to walk out.

"Miguel here will drive you over," the man introduced me to the only Spanish gentleman I had seen at the resort.

"I can walk, it's okay."

"No. You don't walk here. Call us to get to and from your room."

I blinked. I understood now. This is how the other half lived. Everyone was at their beg and call.

"How are you, sir?" Miguel asked me.

"I'm good. How are you doing?" I asked as I got onto the golf cart and we drove off.

"Same, it's a hot one today."

It was. It was over a hundred, but a week alone in the desert, I was used to being drenched in dry heat.

"Yeah, I just got back from camping in the desert."

"Oh, you're one of those guys. We don't get many here."

"Do you guys have good food here?" I wasn't sure what he was implying until I saw all of the old men surrounded by young women with fake tits. I definitely did not feel like I fit in as we drove by the 18+ adult pool which was clearly separated from the family section by a row of suites, a gift shop, and a restaurant.

"Here's your room," Miguel said as I was gazing off at everyone getting ready to party their asses off.

"Thank you, Miguel. I hope you have a great day."

He pulled my bags off and walked them to the

door. I went inside, pulled off my stinking clothes. I hadn't showered since my family left. I drew a bath, and while the water filled up, I turned on the TV. I Figured I'd watch something for the first time in months.

I knew the voice before I saw it as Ice Cube cracked jokes with his uncle. *Friday* was on, and I immediately broke into tears.

Happy birthday, dad.

Sometimes the universe gives us gifts we don't think we deserve. And this was mine on my dad's birthday. A small memory I had lost in time. I sat on the chair and watched it until I heard the water from the bathtub running onto the bathroom floor.

I let the hot water soak my muscles while I prepared myself for the next trip.

I started training. I had a few months to get ready for Yosemite. My eyes were set on Half Dome. An 18 mile round trip hike with 4800ft in elevation gain. It would be the hardest physical thing I ever did and to this day, have ever done.

I loaded a backpack with weights, and started putting miles in as I trekked through New Paltz, and the parks of New York. I wasn't going to fail like I had at Mount Rainier. No, I was going to finish this one.

I started looking up how to prevent altitude sickness. I started thinning my blood with aspirin during the week. It was some random fact I had come across. That by taking it before your trip, and at the first few days before your hike, you could prevent sickness.

Those three months flew by, and before I knew it, I was pulling into Yosemite. As you turn into that park, there's a completely different world to see as you drive around the bend and see El Capitan standing in front of you. It is magnificent. I felt reverence for the first time in my life. I've never used that word to describe anything else. It was pure.

I pulled my rental over. Standing there, I immediately grabbed my phone and took a photo. I felt guilty about it. My memories from Zion had kicked in, and I didn't want to just be a tourist here. I wanted to *live*. Looking back, I wish I took more photos there. I'll go back one day and allow myself to be a tourist.

I set up camp. I'd start my hike in less than 48 hours. That meant I had to prepare. I went to the supermarket in the park, and grabbed everything I needed. Two apples, four protein bars, a gallon of water, and a box of spinach. Yeah, completely unprepared.

I started early. The sun hadn't even risen and I was burning calories and energy too damn fast. I was exhausted by the time I reached the first set of bathrooms. I wasn't prepared for the steep inclines, but I wasn't going to fail this one.

When I reached Nevada Falls, I had already eaten through an apple, and two protein bars. I knew if I was going to keep doing this, the only way I'd finish was by digging deep and pushing myself through what I thought I couldn't do. I trekked on, the blisters on my feet had already grown large and uncomfortable in my hiking sneakers. Some had popped, and others bled.

After I got through another area of quick elevation gain, I started questioning myself.

Why the fuck are you doing this? Just go back to camp. You always give up. That's all you are. A quitter. A liar. Just tell everyone you did it. No one will know. Just go back, you aren't meant to do this.

The path leveled out, and the open trail turned to thick trees. I took my backpack off, sat on a large rock, and contemplated walking back to my camp.

My dad's mother loved butterflies, and at her funeral, everyone broke down crying when a Monarch flew by as we buried her. My dad even commented on it in between his tears and grief.

While I contemplated giving up, I sat alone amongst the trees. I stopped looking at my feet which were slowly breaking, and stared up at the canopy and sky beyond it. Hundreds of Monarchs were dancing in the sun. I think my dad was there that day. I'm still not a godly man, but the universe sure likes to give you signs when you're struggling. Whether it's karma, or just coincidence, there was something there that kept me going. I loaded my backpack, and kept going until I hit the final camp-site before the switchbacks up the side of Half Dome.

If you can't do it for yourself, do it for him. He wouldn't want you to fail.

Yeah, but what about our last conversation?

My mind went quiet, I had no answer to the dichotomy going on inside of me.

The view of Half Dome just before the cables.

The final climb was arduous, but the view was

worth it. As I crested the final hill, I stared off in all directions taking in the scenery and the few photos I gave myself permission to take.

I felt nothing. No pride, no joy. I felt absolutely nothing standing there. I had just done something I didn't think I would finish, and no emotions ran through me.

Now you have to get down.

My blisters had popped and my knees were weak. I only had to go 9 miles back to camp and descend almost 5000 ft with barely any food, and my water running low.

I ran out of water before I got back to Nevada Falls. Everything was sucking again. My stomach was hurting and I ran behind a rock to lose my bowels just like I had done on Mount Rainier.

When I reached camp, I took my backpack off, and went to the supermarket again for a Gatorade, water, and a hot burrito. It was the best tasting thing I have ever eaten in my life. A grocery store burrito.

My tent was my home now, and as I peeled my sock away from my bloody foot, I realized I couldn't feel my big toe anymore. The blister on the side of it was massive, another toe on top of it. I immediately lanced it and let all the pus and liquid free itself from the skin. I pulled the other sock off, and my toenail came with it. I was a mess. I wrapped them the best I could, and said I'd fix it in the morning.

As I lay in my sleeping bag, I tried to figure out why I felt nothing. Just empty. That's all I was.

You've done it. Something way too difficult for you. Now what?

"I'll write a book. That's what I'll do."

That's when *Betta Fish and Backcountry* started. Alone, broken, and empty in a tent in Yosemite.

I was asleep before 8pm.

You really find your worth when you're broken and alone. That night the temperature dropped. I had prepped for forty degree nights, but a cold front blew in at the last minute and I found myself in single digits. I woke up shivering with no energy to move. I reached out of my sleeping bag, and grabbed all my dirty clothes, and sweaters I had packed. I stuffed them in the base of my sleeping bag, then pulled myself in tight making sure to close the gap where my head was with another sweater.

At least you'll stay a little warm tonight.

The next morning, I made my way over to Urgent Care. My blisters had reformed after I lanced them. I couldn't feel most of my left foot, and the pain that shot through my legs up into my hips was some of the worst I'd ever felt.

"I congratulate you for actually lancing these," the nurse said. "Most people would leave them, but they're so bad you want to drain these." She peeled the bandages off my other foot. Blood and pus oozed down my feet as she saw my missing toenails.

"You're going to want to keep this one covered and clean. I'll give you a coupon for a free shower today, but I'll clean it here." She wiped it down with alcohol and the stinging was nothing to the shots of pain going through my lower body.

"What about not feeling anything in half my left foot?"

"Probably a pinched nerve. Just give it time, and when you get home, check in with your Primary."

I wanted to hike El Cap after Half Dome, but I knew my body wasn't going to let that happen. I stuck to the small flat trails near Camp 4 the rest of my trip.

When I got back to New York, my left foot was still numb. I set to rubbing my big toe, calf, and shins until I started to regain feeling. I wouldn't regain full feeling for months.

You deserve this for being so stupid and unprepared.

My old thoughts had come back and I didn't want to travel as much as 2019 came to a close.

I released my first book Black Friday that year.

I was sitting at work when I pulled up the product page on Amazon.

#1 New Release in bright orange stood next to it.

I was speechless.

That has to be wrong. There's no way.

I scrolled down to the categories and there it was clear as day. #1 in three categories.

I did it. I fucking did it. All the people who said you couldn't, shouldn't, and can't. They're all fucking wrong.

The rush of endorphins put me some place else. I was proud for once. My highs were high again, and I maintained that rush to start my second poetry collection immediately.

I had no clue what I was doing, I didn't know about marketing, promotions, ads, or building a mailing list. And I wouldn't understand any of it until *Chasing Lights* crashed and burned. I released it three days before New York shutdown during the pandemic.

I could come up with excuses that the pandemic ruined my release, that I spent too much on a professional book cover, or my book came out too fast. But, I had nothing set up to market, and *Betta Fish* was all luck.

After *Chasing Lights,* I struggled in quarantine deciding if I wanted to continue writing. I didn't see a 10% return on my investment. It's not because of the pandemic, or my cover, or my blurb. I didn't have a plan. Like most of my life, I just went for something, and tried to achieve it, and when I did, I was higher than the stars. Here I was locked in my house alone, and I came crashing down to earth like Icarus with my own failure.

That's maybe a cliched image, but I felt broken again. I didn't want to write anymore. I had achieved something that no one I know had done. And now, I failed to even get the next one off the ground.

You should just give up. Stop writing. No one cares. All your shit is depressing.

I was funneling everything that my friends and coworkers were telling me back at myself. And the worst part, I was starting to believe them. Who wanted to hear someone write about his dead dad anyway? Who wanted to read depressing shit? I stopped writing for me, and worked on the other facet of myself, my science fiction, and that's when the cold slap of reality hit me.

I needed to learn from the mistakes. I needed to make a plan for my books, and my life. I had spent too much time just throwing shit into the wind to see what would take off.

Why do I say this? Because even when I didn't want to, I still got up, and I did the job. Something inside of me wanted that orange sticker again. Something inside of me wanted to share a story, my story, unabashedly.

16

SEATTLE

I MOVED TO SEATTLE IN THE MIDDLE OF THE pandemic. Did nine months out west on the coast looking for my happiness. I found a lonely solitude out there instead. Locked away in a micro-studio, all I could do was work, work on my writing, and play games. In my entire time out there, I saw two people. Whether it be from the pandemic, my NY attitude, or just my demeanor, I didn't fit in. I knew I had to go back to New York when I was making multiple phone calls a day to friends back home.

I was losing it again, that independence I found.

You're a failure. You can't even make it out West by yourself. You need company. You need to feel connected to people. And you can't even make new friends out here.

Hard stop.

Mount Rainier National Park. I spent a lot of time outside when I couldn't stand my own company

I packed up my car one morning when I couldn't stand my own company anymore, and I drove back East. Through the Rockies and the flat parts of Montana. My music blaring, and my eyes set on change.

If you're going to go back, make sure you're worth coming back to.

I wasn't. I was lost in my head, and didn't feel like I was anything special. Scared, alone, dependent on my girlfriend living on the other side of the country for my own happiness, I wanted to feel a closeness and warmth to anyone besides myself.

Something in me changed when I came back to New York, just as something changed when I left. Maybe it was the breakup once I returned home, maybe it was the want to not feel like an utter human waste, or the want to not be depressed. Maybe it was all the conversations I had with my father on that lonely fifty-hour car ride. After all, it was just him, me, the open road, and whatever music I could put on. Probably a culmination of all of the above.

Coming back here, I resolved myself to actually working through the demons I faced in my life. Rather than sweep them under the rug, I put all the moments that made me scared, resentful, complacent, suicidal, and downright angry on paper. They're all in front of you, and me. I cried, a lot, laughed, smiled, and at times, felt the peace I was always looking for and only ever tasted in my travels. I've made a home in that dark room I was running from, and now my demons have to face me, because I'm not letting them control my life anymore. It's cliche, but it's true nonetheless.

I've taken ownership of everything that happened to me that I used as an excuse to act the way I did.

Everything molded me to be here today. And

every way I acted set me up for this—set me up to write this book. This is my love letter to those demons. A love letter to the life I hated for so long. This is letting go so I can be the person I want to be, rather than the person I was, and am.

17
DAD'S APARTMENT

THE THING WITH DEPRESSION, IT'S ADDICTING. IT'S easy to stay there, cause eventually it becomes your home. It becomes your "normal." Your baseline for the day is feeling like absolute fucking shit. Staying in bed becomes easy, and getting up to brush your teeth becomes the hardest thing to do.

I've been working on fighting all those demons, burning them on the pages in front of me for relief, but more importantly, accepting them. Because every one of them is me. And I have to accept that. I had to unpack my life to make it easier to carry.

I signed up to start doing Jiu Jitsu again. And I knew I had to, because the gym is directly across from my dad's apartment. I hadn't gone by it in over a year. Every time I would try, I'd find another way to any destination just to avoid passing by.

You don't have to do this. Just go home. Don't drive by his place today.

I drove to Jiu Jitsu that first morning back, and struggled every second to not just turn around and go home, wallow in myself because I was sad about a breakup. My dad's birthday was only two days away and I'd have to drive right by his apartment. As I pulled into the parking lot for class, I still thought about pulling out.

I have to do this, otherwise I won't get better.

I dug deep in myself. I had work to do. And for the first time, the work was for myself, and no one else.

I'm alone in my mind. If I'm gonna be saved, I'm going to do it myself.

I wanted to vomit passing by his apartment taking deep breaths to not break down.

I parked my car and went inside.

I did my class while fighting all those incessant thoughts, and got my ass kicked like I knew I would. I walked out feeling good about myself for the first time in years.

Once I got back in my car, waved goodbye to everyone, and made the right turn onto Route 9, I broke down. As I passed by his apartment again, I bawled. Not cried. Not shed a tear. I full on sobbed. Tears and snot ran down my face as I drove by. I was proud and sad all at once. I did something I had no wish to do, but I was hurting more than I told anyone or let them see.

I struggled at the most basic task, keeping my hands on the steering wheel, the car in a straight line. I balanced a vape in my right hand between two fingers. I grabbed my phone off the dash of my car at the first red light and sent a text to my mom.

I'M SORRY I WASN'T NICE THIS MORNING. I'M STRUGGLING. I MISS DAD, AND EVERYTHING HURTS.

1 8

ON GOOD MEMORIES

I BURIED A LOT OF MEMORIES, EVEN THE GOOD ONES. I felt I didn't deserve them, that because of the way I had treated my dad at the end of his life, I was undeserving of enjoying any memory that brought a smile to my mind. Therapy brought some of those memories back.

You don't get to live here. This is a place for good people to live. And you aren't a good person.

He had that green Monte Carlo, with purple tints that he installed himself. The back left window wasn't perfect, and there was always a stream of light that hit the backseats.

One Tuesday, we drove to get groceries, and when we got back to his apartment, Ozzy's "Dreamer" was playing. He said to me, "Nicholas, it's just me and you against the world. Just two dreamers who want better days."

After he died, and that song came on, I couldn't finish it. I still have never fully listened to it since.

It was me and you against the world. Now that you're gone, it's just me. You were stolen from us at 54. Now who do I call when I need to be a man?

When I was twelve, or thirteen, he had gotten his settlement from breaking his back on the job. He bought a Hummer H2, and took me on vacation for the first time. It was a Disney cruise down in Florida.

He spent most of the time in the suite, watching TV, and chasing pills with water while I was up in the arcade playing a Jurassic Park video game.

We lived on room service pizza that I can still taste to this day. Gooey, loaded with sauce, and not cooked all the way through. I loved it.

When we got to Key West, we took our photo of the most southern point in the United States, held parrots, and went to the Ernest Hemingway House before we rented a jet ski.

I was terrified of the water, still am. But I clung to his life vest as we soared through the waves. I remember the taste of the crystal blue ocean in my eyes. Stinging and happy.

Dad and I on vacation.

When we returned to New York, and winter came, he told me to get in the Hummer. It was a bad snowstorm that day, and we drove by the house him and my mother shared before we moved to my grandmother's. The park hadn't been plowed at all.

He drove right over the parking lot and into the grass and started drifting the truck while 80's hair metal played in the background. It's one of the few times I genuinely laughed with him as the truck gripped the ground and spun in circles.

19
"RECOVERY"

IN THE DARK ROOM
    That I was trying so hard to escape from,
    I'll make a home.
    Now all my demons
    Have to deal with me.

Nicholas Trieste
June 18, 2021

20

PRAYERS

I'VE PRAYED TO DIE. SAID TO WHATEVER LIES OUT there: beyond this planet, that I didn't want to live, and to just take me in my sleep.

Whatever light is inside me, or whatever good fortune you have planned for me, please give it to someone else. I'm undeserving of it. Let someone else enjoy the life you have planned for me, and take me tonight.

I've never shared that with anyone. Not my family, not my friends, not anyone I've ever dated. I never wanted to break their hearts, to know that I've been so low, that I had no wish to be a part of their worlds anymore.

I've survived the alcohol, the not eating, and the over-eating, the depression. There has to be a reason for that, because my body should have given up on

84

me too many times and I wanted to give up on myself just as many. I'm still here. Still fighting those mental issues that no one wants to bring up, that people are scared to share because of the stigma behind them.

"No one wants to talk to someone who's depressed."

"You're unstable."

"You need to be institutionalized."

"You need to be put on drugs. Someone needs to put you in a room, and throw away the key."

I've added all these things people have said to me to the pile of things I carry, and what I use to prove them wrong. They drive me to be better. But, I've also thought that maybe every single one of them was right. Maybe I am unstable and no one wants to talk to me. Maybe the drugs are the only key. Every day I wake up and live to prove them wrong.

You're no one.

I never want to be on those pills to make me feel like my life is okay. I'm vehemently against them. Because if I need drugs to feel alive, then I don't want to be alive. I want to be *me*. I'm chasing that happiness, and self-acceptance, so when I do find it, I can stand proud knowing that I've gone against everything they've said to me.

Jiu-Jitsu, running, working out, and writing

about these bad thoughts helps. The people who reach out to me, saying they've gone through the same thing, or feel the same way, they're the ones who drive me to be better and more open. There's a kindness knowing you've helped someone. There's a good feeling in knowing that someone is reaching out to you to share their life with you.

Those are the things that keep me going, in the face of all that hate, and all the hate I have for myself.

I wake up every day with everything I've been through, and done. Now, I accept them, and I know where I've failed and sucked at being a good person. There's a silence in that acceptance, while the mind is swirling. I get to look at everything and see how far I've come. Some days fucking suck, but accepting things, and making changes to actually change, there's a freedom there. Some people may never get that, because it's easy to stay in your pain, and the hard part is to work through it, and put it on display for the world.

I don't make apologies for my story; I only apologize for the relationships I've ruined because of my own insecurities. And to my father for what happened out of anger.

The bullying, the drugs, the alcohol, the father who was in and out of my life, they're just what I was handed. I can't blame the world for my issues. That's what I've always done. My issues are my own, and recognizing that my issues are directly my fault for my responses to them is where that silence lies.

What do I want to leave behind?

It's the thought I have now. What do I want to be? How do I want to be remembered? I don't want to be remembered as angry, depressed, anxious, an alcoholic, a shitty friend, a bad boyfriend.

I want to be remembered as an honest man. Someone who spoke his truth even when no one wanted to hear it. I want to be remembered as someone who was always there when someone was in the lowest place of their life. I want to be remembered as a best friend, a phenomenal boyfriend, and one of the most genuine people you'd ever meet. Those are my goals. Every day, those are what I want to be. And I fail—a lot. That's when the brutal honesty I now have with myself comes in. If I can't be honest with myself and my failures, I can't be honest for anyone else.

I've lost so much, including myself. I always pivoted to find a solution to everything that came my way, but it took me 28 years to realize I was the problem, and the only way I'd find peace was to go through my life with a fine-tooth comb, put it on paper, and fix myself. I had to acknowledge everything I'd been through was my fault because of how I let it mold me. I'm not saying what happened was my fault, but my reactions to them are entirely my own.

That's what this book is about at the end of the day. Shedding light on my darkest places, and putting it out for the world to see. I'm human, and I've royally fucked up. This is me owning everything I am, was, and will be.

I SEE 8S AT EVERY CORNER. THE INTERNET SAYS IT'S my "Angel Number." That I'm on the right path, that I have to embrace it and push through this.

4/30

I am someone who doesn't ask for help. But today I did.

5/1

888. Make the changes in your life to be the person you were destined to. I'm going to fall further than I ever have. I know that. The lows are going to be the lowest ever. Am I ready for this? Am

I ready to face myself? I am not a bad person, only misguided. If I put the time into this, I will come out the other side. Am I ready for that? Am I ready to face myself? I don't think so, but I have to do it. I have to look at myself in the mirror and let the 8's guide me.

5/2

Embody kindness. Embody a life worth living. Embody the man you want to be, the man you <u>must</u> be.

5/3

Start trusting. Start being sincere to everyone you meet. Work to be better than you were a minute ago. Do better. <u>Do fucking better!</u>

I feel empty this morning, numb, like there's nothing in my heart and I have no soul. The silence has been terrifying, and deafening. I'm unsure what to believe in anymore. Is this my figurative death? I don't wanna be like this. I don't wanna be like this. I don't wanna be like this.

5/3 (NIGHT)

I felt a shift in my mindset while meditating.

Rubbing my fingers together, the creases of my fingerprints against each other like sandpaper. Become examined and the examiner all at once.

Become the eye of the storm when life rages on around you. Become the foundation for everything you ever wanted, and be the foundation for everyone around you. If I get through this, I will be something different, something new, something bright.

5/4

Massive self-doubt today. Insecurities rising up. Bad relationships. Guilt clouds my mind. <u>Feel like a failure</u>.

5/5

I am struggling with suicidal thoughts and depression. I want to drink everything away. I want to hide again.

5/6

Go easy on yourself today. It'll work out like it's supposed to. One day you'll make it through this unbearable weight of guilt and pain. Continue facing my hell.

. . .

5/7/21

Empty. That's how I feel today looking through my memories while meditating. A lone, cold teardrop ran down my face holding all the joy of the memories that I miss.

I will be better. I am better than I was a week ago. Next week I will be better than I am today.

5/8

I touched my soul last night. It looked and felt like a blue cube/sphere. That connectedness to myself, and all that I'll be and become. Calm, cool, collected, relaxed all at once. Choose your actions with intent.

5/9

Don't give up on people just because they give up on you! Don't give up on yourself either.

5/9

It's time to begin again at any and every moment. As much as I want to extinguish that flame in me, that burning I feel at every moment, I can't. I need to use that cold fusion as fuel. Burn brighter, burn hotter than everyone around me. Leave a scorched earth. A legacy worth talking about that no one can touch.

5/9

Own your thoughts and faults no matter what. Apologize honestly, and say what you truly feel with conviction no matter how fucked up you feel.

Live and live with intent.

5/9 (NIGHT)

I let pain, loneliness, jealousy, envy, guilt and suspicion become my personality traits. It's unacceptable and ruins me. None of these are what I want to be, and I will kill them off.

I am capable, ambitious, and loving. Negative traits can no longer drive my decisions in life.

5/10

Day ten of meditation and self-reflection. I don't feel good this morning looking through the old photos in my hands and head. They're a moment in time—fleeting. Things I will never get back.

Today won't be like this morning. It will be better

and I will push through to find that bright light. Become better, be better. Do better for yourself first. Then apply it to everyone around you.

Be uncompromising with myself. I am a tyrant of my soul, it is not a tyrant of me. Better days, forever and always.

Who do I want to be?

5/11

Deep regret for the person I was that ruined everything. I am better than I was, and I will continue to put in the work.

5/13

I am clingy to the point of driving people away. I need to work on this, my emotions need direction rather than outbursts. Consistency, integrity, honesty.

5/14

All I did was dream of her last night.

5/15

I feel nothing.

· · ·

5/16

I can't build a home in someone else's chest.

5/17

Where do I exist in this world?

5/18

Genuineness. Be genuine, always. Make today the turning point in your life. For yourself, and everyone around you. You are not a broken man. Go to hell, and don't turn back. Today you will push through it. Keep going, keep pushing, keep thriving. You got this, now, forever, always.

5/19

I got this.

5/21

I am alone in the dark room of my mind. All those aspects of me, I have to accept them and change who I want to be and need to be for myself, and no one else. I am my own worst enemy, and I can't be that person any longer.

. . . .

5/25

I am at war with my heart, soul, and mind. To stop the depression and bad thoughts that cloud my mind.

5/26

In order to become something special, I have to leave something special behind.

5/27

I am losing the fight. This unbearable weight is crushing me and becoming too much to carry. Why am I doing this to myself? To be better. I have to keep reminding myself of that.

5/28

I have to make it through this. Be relentless, and keep going through hell. Honesty, integrity, compassion. No compromising with my mind.

5/30

Today during meditation I went somewhere else. Somewhere "in" or "beside" myself. I knew I had a body, and felt my blood coursing through a beating heart. I am not this at the same time. I have hands that I feel, but they aren't mine. That's not the right way to describe it, but this "me" is something else from my body.

6/3

Speak your truth when your hearts hurts, chest caves, and voice cracks. At least go to sleep knowing you did your best while burning.

6/6 (DAD's birthday)

I visited my grandma's gravestone today. I spread his ashes out there. I haven't been back since 2017. I didn't say much of anything, just let the wind blow. Cried and asked for guidance. I want to be better. Is facing my demons really worth it? Everything hurts right now.

6/7

I am terrified to put myself on display to the world with this book. Is it worth it? All these terrible parts of me for everyone to see? I know I haven't been a good person at times in my life. If I was, I wouldn't have blocked him before he died. I would have tried to hash things out one more time. Is it worth writing all of this down? My sins for the world to judge.

6/9

I opened that calendar today. The one with the cat on it. I haven't opened it since before the pandemic. I should include it in the book. A stamp for my life. Let everyone see what I live with. Guilt written in stone.

6/10

I have to start loving myself and my faults.

6/11

By fighting myself these last two months, no one can hurt me. Is this peace? There's still more work to do. I can't get comfortable here. There's work to do every day. Forever. Be better than I was yesterday, every day.

6/12

I'm losing friends, cutting ties with people I thought I cared about. I can't let the toxicity in. I can't continue being the person they think I still am.

. . .

6/13

I want to call my dad today. Show him all the things I've accomplished. I want to make him proud. Are you proud?

6/14

Reinvent yourself. Be something better, something rare in this world. Honesty, integrity, compassionate. Brutal when needed, especially with myself.

6/16

People always told me to be small. I liked being small in my life, unseen by those around me. I was able to hide who I was, and I kept avoiding myself. Now I'm trying to live loud every day and people I considered friends hate me for it. Good. I'll live large and loud every fucking day.

6/18

I'm going to finish this book, cement something in this world. I don't want to. But I <u>need</u> to.

. . .

6/20

I've been sleeping through the nights. This is a win for me.

LETTERS TO MY FATHER

RICH,

IT'S SAID that rain falls on the just and unjust as well. Lord knows you had your share of rain. You should know that your time here mattered. Not only did you take on the most noble profession and did a great job, but you also left your legacy in your children.

Through all the turmoil, somehow the message got through loud and clear to your children. Nick has a solid philosophy and a dedicated plan for his life. I've had the honor to talk to him about his writing and his plans. It is abundantly clear that your influence has created a desire in him to succeed in all his endeavors. I know you are looking down on him and all of your children with great pride.

On a personal note, I want you to know that I always thought of you as my little brother. I was proud when you told me you wanted to follow in my footsteps and become a police officer. I was honored to be your supervisor for a short period of time, even though we banged heads many times.

Although things got rough toward the end of your short life, I never stopped seeing you as the little brother I knew, loved and was proud of. I want to share with you one more time the poem I kept in my vest all those years. (You knew the significance).

I want to remind you that it wasn't your fault for the way your father treated you. Think back to the laminated poem I carried in my bulletproof vest, the one my mother gave me.

"You'll be a man, my son."

-UNCLE JOEY
    June 21, 2021

Toys for Tots with Uncle Joey

RICHARD,

I WRITE this letter with tears pouring down my cheeks.

I want to start off by saying I am so sorry for the way things happened and ended between us. I don't know how to handle it.

My heart was ripped to shreds when I got that phone call that you passed away. I live with so much pain and regret on a daily basis for not speaking to you before you passed away.

I want you to know that I didn't get the message you wanted me to call you until the day you passed away. (Rather the day we found you). You were gone before we knew. I am sickened that you died alone and in so much emotional torment.

I wish you were here, to give me advice—to make me laugh until my cheeks and stomach hurt. I'm writing you this letter hoping it will give me some comfort, but I don't think that will happen. Had I gotten that message, we could have talked and hugged it out.

I never told you, you were more than my big brother, you were my friend and father figure. You were who I had growing up. Stood by me and believed me, held my hand while they examined me.

Remember Bill's Pizzeria? Mommy would call

you and say, "Rich, she did it again!" You would come to Bill's in the police car, I'd run to the back until my friends ratted me out. You took me home and said, "Stop it, Shelly!" I would say, "Same place in an hour, Rich." How much I miss those days, what I wouldn't give to have them back. I miss your advice, your knowledge, and quotes.

-"The one who makes you cry is never worth your tears."

-"Silence speaks volumes."

Phil and I speak of you often. I love hearing his stories about you and him on the job, it makes me feel closer to you. Sometimes I feel like you're near.

Krystal is an amazing mom, and a replica of you. Nicholas is doing big things, and he's the reason I have this opportunity to write you. Nico and Christian are around. I wish you could have held on a bit longer to see them.

Visit me in my dreams, Rich. I miss you. Until we meet again big brother, I will keep you in my soul.

I love you more than all the words in all the books in all the world.

LOVE FOREVER AND ALWAYS,
Baby sis, Shelly.
June 19, 2021.

RICHARD,

THESE ARE JUST some of my thoughts. I have so many memories. Our late night talks, texting all the time. (I still have some of them). From going to English-town to race, to you in my living room playing "I just died in your arms tonight"—dancing around.

You said I was your angel, then you bought me two ceramic angels. I still have them where you put them.

I remember you coming by my house just blasting music out of your stereo.

When you were in your coma, I stayed at the hospital. When you came out, you asked me, "why did you fight so hard for me?" I said, "for your children." The look of pure love came over your face. You said your children are your world and came to stay with me after.

I remember cooking you dinner, and you'd hide it under the couch so Brittany would make you a grilled cheese. When I found out, you said, "she made me eat it!"

Taking you to the doctor, driving down the highway the song Sweet Cherry Love came on. You turned it up so loud I almost crashed. You scared the crap out of me! All you could say was that you liked that song.

You would always have a cup of coffee for me when I came home from work. It was cold, but you still had it for me.

Your children are amazing. I enjoy talking to them, and seeing them. Nicholas and Krystal come by my job to see me. They are so special. Your grandson is such a little man—very smart. When I see your children and what they have become, you would be so proud of them. I miss you, Richard.

-DEANNA
June 20, 2021

Deanna and Dad. A photo he kept.

MY DEAR BROTHER RICHARD,

WE HAVE SHARED many great conversations where we agreed to disagree; and disagree we did. Yet in the end, we always respected each other's point of view and loved each other. You always said to me, "why do you have to be the voice of reason?" I was never able to answer that question except to say that it's who I am. You would be happy to know that I am still the voice of reason and hopefully that voice continues to impact others positively.

The day that I received the phone call that you died was unbelievable. It is still hard to believe that you are no longer physically here. I know that your spirit is here and will continue to live on through the many memories we all have, as well as through the lives of your children and grandson.

You were always supportive of me and I love and appreciate you for that. You were there for the special times in my life: walking and pulled me down the aisle (lol), my graduation, the godfather to my son, Jason, and also Jordan.

I recall when you were in the hospital in a coma. It was Deanna's birthday and you had not been responsive. Deanna and I were in the room talking to you and I told you to wish her a Happy Birthday. You then opened your eyes and looked at her. That made us so happy. We started crying. By the way, I planned to take her to Niagara Falls for her birthday, but you gave her (and all of us) such a better gift—opening your eyes.

You are missed and loved very much. I miss your humor and sarcasm—even though sometimes it was annoying.

God knew what his plan was. You used to tell me you wanted to go to church with me. I am sorry we never got to do that. How perfect it was, God's plan that you found a Bible of mine from when I was a teenager. Neither of us could have imagined that would happen.

My dearest brother, I miss you very much. I am grateful you are no longer in pain and suffering. You deserve the peace. I am so thankful that I have this opportunity to write you this letter.

ALL MY LOVE, your sister,
Wendy Ann
"The Voice of Reason"
June 27, 2021

Dad, Poppy, and Wendy at her graduation 1983

"Silence is the ultimate weapon and the hardest argument to dispute."

-Rich Turner

DEAR DAD,

I'm sorry.

I'm sorry that you had nothing but my silence when you left us. I never wanted to hurt you...

I was at work when the State Troopers called me. I don't usually answer numbers I don't recognize, but somehow instinctively I knew to answer this one. Deep down I knew it was something to do with you and I knew it wasn't good. I managed to hold it together until I called Aunt Deanna and heard her voice. I maintained my composure up until that point and I'm not sure how. In hindsight, I was in shock but at the same time it wasn't entirely unexpected. Your health hadn't been that great and no matter how much I pleaded with you to keep your appointments with the doctor, you were always distracted by something else.

The days after that are a blur and I don't remember much. I remember sitting at the table with the funeral director. I was irrationally angry at the fact that I had to sit there as life went on for everyone else outside those walls, while mine was at a standstill. I was angry at everyone who came up to Nicholas and I, telling us how sorry they were. How dare they be sorry for us when their lives get to continue on after they leave the funeral home. The devastation I felt (and still feel) cannot be put into words.

I still can't process what happened and I don't think I'll ever be able to come to terms with it. I wish you were there to see me get married. Yes, Chris and I finally got married. We played Motley Crue, Def Leppard and our first dance was a Foreigner song. You would have probably taken over as the DJ at some point and it would have been all Freestyle from there. You would have have been the life of the party. I dedicated "Spring Love" to you at the reception. That was the last time I've been able to listen to it. I keep it on my playlist, but I can only listen to it momentarily before I have to skip to the next song.

It took me a while to stop picking up my phone to call you whenever I needed advice. I think that's the hardest part. You're not just a phone call away anymore. I remember all of your advice and whenever I'm faced with a difficult situation or decision, I always think of you and what your advice would be. I'm doing my best to live up to your expectations. You always told me "never let anyone break your fucking spirit" and I won't. I'm trying to teach Sean this as well. I refuse to let anyone walk all over me and I will always stand up for myself. I'm still learning, but I promise you I'll always be the take no shit kind of woman you were so proud of me for being.

Remember when I used to cut class in High School? You'd pull up to the curb, your music impossibly loud. I was embarrassed. My friends would laugh and tell me I was in trouble. Somehow I'd hear your voice above the noise: "Krystal Nicole get back to class!" I could never get away with anything. Everyone knew you - knew I was your daughter. The teachers would threaten to tell you about my cutting class, trying to scare me by telling me that they knew my father. To this day I still meet people who knew you. Who remember me when I was a child. Some of them offer apologies and some of them have no idea that you're gone. It's always awkward when they apologize. I never know what to say...

You'd be so proud of Sean. At any given time he's easily the smartest person in the room. He's kind, he's caring and he always has a joke to tell. When he makes certain expressions he looks just like you. I can only imagine the discussions you would have with him. I wish you guys had more time together. I always tell him you're watching over him and although he didn't have very long with you, he still has some memory of you. I'm grateful for that.

I feel unimaginable guilt over us not speaking before you died. I hope you have forgiven me, because I don't think I'll ever be able to forgive myself.

I put off writing this letter because I feel like I can't put all of these emotions into words. I feel like I can't do your memory justice. You were someone who lived life passionately. Whether good or bad, there was no gray area for you. You either loved it or you hated it. Life hadn't always been kind to you, but you never let it stop you. You got knocked down and sometimes you had to stay down for a bit, but you never let those things define you. You and I didn't always get along and I'm so sorry for anything I ever said that made you feel something other than the respect, love and admiration I have for you. I'm honored to have had you as my Dad.

Love,
    "Bright Eyes"
    Krystal
    July 2, 2021

Krystal and Dad at Kindergarten Graduation 1990

DEAR DAD,

THIS LETTER HAS BEEN years in the making, and I'm not sure how I should start it. If you were sitting in front of me, and I had still gone through all of this, I'd like you to know I do and did truly love you. Everyone says I look like you, it's the look in our eyes. The mirror shows me a pain and a determination, though I'm not sure that's what everyone else sees. I see someone broken who wants to build something better. I'm going to build something better.

I was very angry with you, hateful at times. I didn't understand what loneliness you felt, but I think now, I understand it better. I've been at the lowest points of my life since you left. Found myself with no company other than my mind.

I think you'd be proud and disappointed that I followed in your footsteps along the way. Able to kick bad habits, and always brush myself off even when I didn't want to. There's that *something* in me that I haven't been able to put words to. A want for a better life, a want to leave behind a legacy worth sharing, a want to be better than I was yesterday. Some kind of fire in me to strive for.

I have a lot of dreams and aspirations I'm

working towards. I want to turn my sci-fi novels into a TV series. I want to be a New York Time's Best Seller. I want to compete in a Jiu-Jitsu tournament and win gold. I want to own a home. I want to be the person people come to when they're struggling. I want to crush whatever life throws at me, so at the end of all things, whatever is out there really says "I threw everything at you, and you would absolutely not stay down, even when you wanted to," as I stand there broken, bruised, and scarred, but never beaten. I'm going to accomplish all of this, because that's what you would have wanted, and it's what I need to do so I can sleep better at night. 110%. Always. With everything I do. No compromise with myself.

You set a perfection in me that I really didn't appreciate growing up, because I thought I was never enough for you. I took that out on myself, and found I wasn't enough for the most important person in my life, me.

I made a promise when you died that I would find the boys. I kept that promise. I know you'd be proud of that. It took me a long time, but I found them. Put them in touch with the family, and hopefully one day soon we're going to meet for the first time since she took them and fled South. I'll do my best to steer them right, let them grow, flourish in this life, and be there when they inevitably fall down. I promise you that, and I promise them that.

The nightmares have mostly stopped, though sometimes they creep back in on me. Your birthday and Father's Day are usually pretty rough, but this year, working on myself, writing this book, and accepting I can't change what happened, but only change what I do today and tomorrow has helped me. I think that realization has allowed me sleep better at night. I'm not going to fall back into my old ways: continuing to run from the things that hurt me or I'm scared to look in the face.

There's a lot of arguments we had, and a lot of times we didn't speak.

I try to remember you fondly, but I can't say we had many good memories. Maybe the time we built a snowman in Peekskill and I gave him a stick for a cigarette is up on that good memory list—something I left out of this book. There's a handful in this brain that I still haven't shared or uncovered. And more than enough bad memories to last a lifetime.

Wherever you are, watching me, get ready for the next chapters. Cause the period at the end of this one hurt, a lot. That dark tunnel I was in, I think it's finally ending. I can't wait to see what the light brings, even if I have to become it and carry it myself.

· · ·

Bʏᴇ, Dad.
    Nicholas Trieste Turner
    June 19, 2021

My favorite photo of us

NOTES

Please consider leaving a review, sharing this on social media, or with your family and friends. The reviews help me greatly, and they keep the dream of making this my full-time job an achievable goal.

ACKNOWLEDGMENTS

I want to thank my best friend, Dylan. Thank you for picking up the phone every night my soul wanted to leave my body.

Thank you to my uncle Shaun for hearing me out as I sobbed at 3am while I went through my hardest breakup. Your words rang in my ears, and I wouldn't have even tried to get my shit straight if you didn't hand me that red book.

Thank you for all the friends who believe in me and continue to buy my books knowing that there's going to be some rough shit in them. You're all real ones.

Thank you to my sister, Krystal. I hope this gives you some closure. I'm sorry our relationship sucked for years. I was clearly going through things I didn't understand and didn't know how to talk about them.

Thank you to my mom for always being there when you could. I'm sorry I wasn't the best son every day, but I try to be better every day since dad left.

Thank you to Diego for pestering me enough to get back into Jiu Jitsu.

Thank you, Mike, and everyone at Black Hole Jiu Jitsu for making me feel like family. It's one of the few things that keeps me level-headed and helps my mental health.

Thank you to Chuck for doing my book cover.

Thank you to Jeremiah for taking the photos and creating it (even if you spilled alcohol on one of his papers, hahah). Really though, it's definitely not a problem.

Thank you to my marketer, Jay, for helping me make this a banger. "To the fucking moon!"

Thank you to my brothers. I'm glad I found you. I wavered a lot in those months that I searched for you. But, I'll always be here. I promised dad I would be, and I promise you that. Men don't break their promises.